YOUR SENSATIONAL SENSE OF SIGHT

BY JULIA VOGEL • ILLUSTRATED BY ROBERT SQUIER

The Child's World

Published by The Child's World®
1980 Lookout Drive • Mankato, MN 56003-1705
800-599-READ • www.childsworld.com

ACKNOWLEDGMENTS
The Child's World®: Mary Berendes, Publishing Director
The Design Lab: Design and production
Red Line Editorial: Editorial direction

LIBRARY OF CONGRESS CATALOGING-IN-PUBLICATION DATA
Vogel, Julia.
  Your sensational sense of sight / by Julia Vogel;
illustrated by Robert Squier.
     p. cm.
  Includes bibliographical references and index.
  ISBN 978-1-60954-287-0 (library bound : alk. paper)
  1. Vision—Juvenile literature. 2. Eye—Juvenile literature. I. Squier,
Robert, ill. II. Title.
  QP475.7.V64 2011
  612.8'4—dc22   2010037845

Printed in the United States of America
Mankato, MN
December, 2010
PA02068

ABOUT THE AUTHOR

Julia Vogel looks near and far for fun science facts. An award-winning author, she has a bachelor's degree in biology and a doctorate in forestry. Julia's favorite sights to see are snowy mountains, hummingbirds, and kids climbing trees.

ABOUT THE ILLUSTRATOR

Robert Squier has been drawing ever since he could hold a crayon. Today, instead of using crayons, he uses pencils, paint, and the computer. Robert lives in New Hampshire with his wife, Jessica, and a dog named "Q."

I'm Rainbow. My friends say I brighten up their lives. Do you like to see me in the sky after rainstorms, too? What else do you like to see?

Seeing is a truly powerful sense. But what is a sense? And how do we see? I'm going on a sightseeing tour to find out more. Come along!

HI!

3

COO-COO!
CHIRP! Birds tweet in the treetops.

MMMM. The smell of sizzling pancakes fills the air.

OH! Light beams into your tent.

These sounds, smells, and sights tell you it's morning at your camp.

Hearing, smelling, and seeing are senses. Tasting and touching are, too. These five senses let you know what's happening around you.

Your senses tell you about the world.

OVER THERE! I spy a blue butterfly.

LOOK OUT! Stay away from that prickly cactus.

Special parts of your body collect sense information. Then they send it to your brain. Your ears, nose, skin, and tongue are all **sense organs**. But my favorite sense organ lets you see everything around you—from bright stars in the sky to the green grass under your toes. It's the incredible eye!

Have you ever wondered why you have two eyes? Try this test to find out.

Hold your arms in front of you with a pencil in each hand. Shut one eye. Now try to touch the pencil ends to each other. Tough, huh? Try again with both eyes open. Is it easier?

Each eye looks at objects from different angles. This helps you figure out how far away things are. Without this skill, you would have trouble catching a baseball.

Let's zoom in to see how your eyes work. Look at one of your eyes in a mirror. See the black circle in the middle? That's your **pupil**. This small opening lets light into your eye. That's the first step in seeing.

Too much light could hurt your eyes. But don't worry—your eyes have their own protection. The colored part of your eye is the **iris**. Its muscles change the size of your pupil. In sunshine, your pupil gets smaller and lets in less light. When it's darker, your iris makes your pupil bigger. What a bright idea!

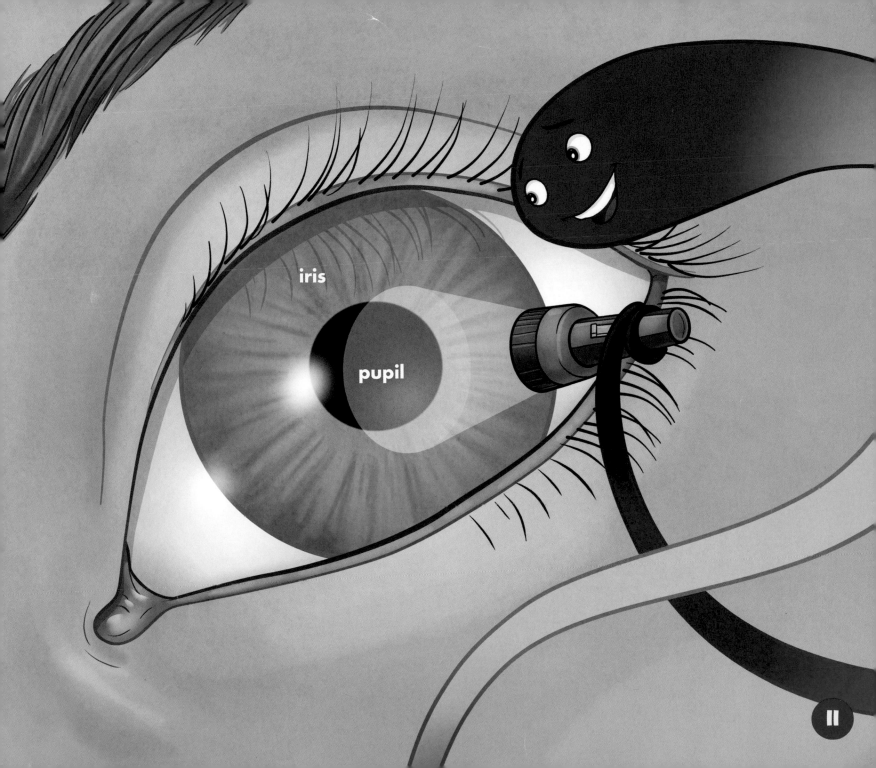

Light bounces off the things you look at. Then it travels to your eyes. But they need to **focus** for you to see clearly.

To focus, each eye bends light. First, light passes through the **cornea**. This see-though eye cover bends the light toward the inside of your eye.

Rays then pass through a clear **lens** that bends them even more. A camera lens also bends light to focus it. But you have to switch camera lenses to bend the light the right amount. The lens in your eye changes shape to focus.

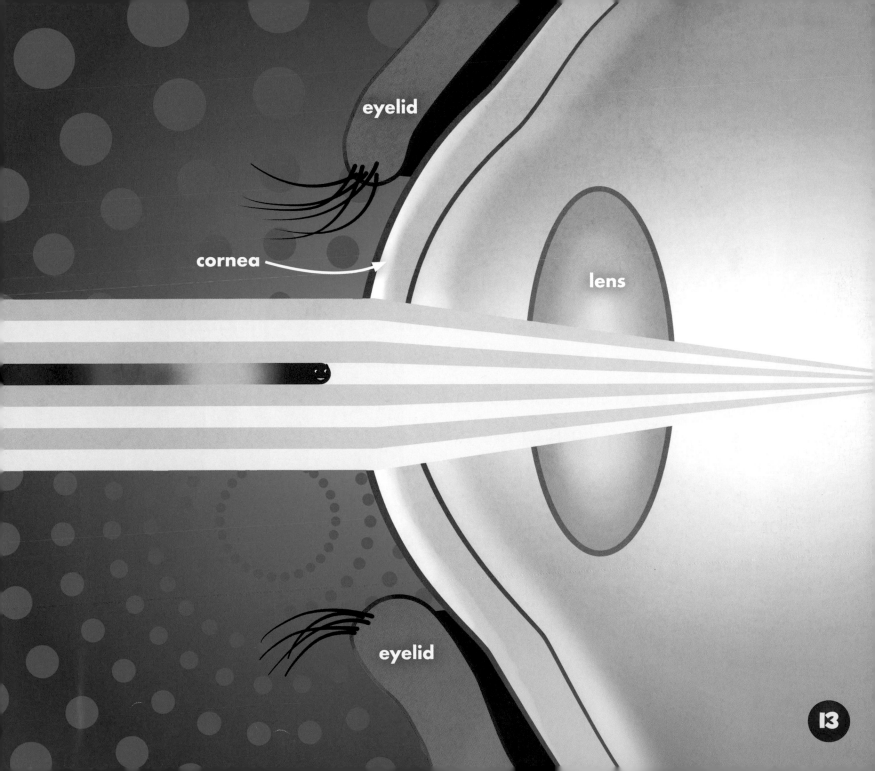

Next comes a crossroads. Rays cross each other before reaching the back of the eyeball. The criss-cross flips the image of whatever you're looking at. When light from this page hits the back of your eye, the words appear upside down.

The light lands on the **retina**. This spot is about the size of a quarter. Your retinas are packed with **sensors** that react to light. Each retina has more than 126 million of them! It's worth a closer look.

eyelid

eyeball

lens

cornea

retina

eyelid

We have to say goodbye to the eye to discover how we see. Why? Seeing really happens in your brain.

At your retina, sight sensors turn light into messages. These messages travel along pathways called **nerves**. The messages go to the sight center of the brain. This part figures out shapes and colors. It figures out distances, too. Your brain lets you know there's a black dog about five feet away.

And, can you believe it? All this happens in less than the blink of an eye!

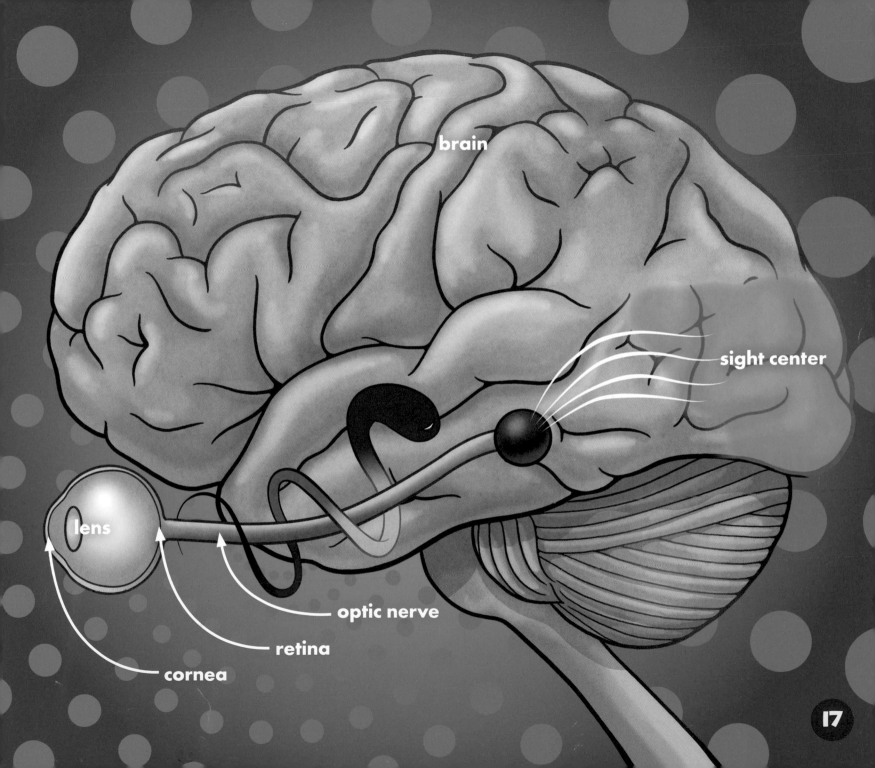

brain

sight center

lens

optic nerve

retina

cornea

Time to move on and explore your everyday life. How is seeing important to you? What you see can make you happy.

 There's your favorite cousin getting off the plane.

 That was the most exciting race ever.

Some sights can be warnings.

DON'T TOUCH! That vine with three leaves is poison ivy.

GET INDOORS! Those dark clouds mean a storm is coming.

Whenever your eyes are open, they're on the lookout for danger.

WOW!

Seeing also helps people understand each other, or **communicate**. People use hand signals to say "Hello" and "Come here." The fans at your football game know what team you're on from your uniform. Signs announce when stores are open or having a sale.

We rely on our eyes to learn, also. Teachers solve math problems on the board at the front of the room. They write classroom rules on posters, too. Watching others helps you learn how to paint, dance, or ski. Reading is another great way to learn by using your eyes.

36 ÷ 6 = 6

Sometimes problems occur with a person's sense of sight. He or she may become nearsighted. This means faraway things look blurry. And some people are farsighted—objects that are close look blurry. People who are nearsighted and farsighted wear glasses or contact lenses to help them see.

More serious eye problems can cause blindness. Head injuries or some illnesses can take away part or all of a person's vision. Some people are born blind, too.

People can live well without eyesight. They can enjoy books by touching patterns of dots. The dots are part of a writing system called **Braille**. Specially trained dogs also help. These dogs guide their owners inside their houses and out in the world.

Your sight is a precious thing. So, protecting it is important. Wear a bike helmet when you're riding around. Wear goggles if you're near harsh chemicals that could splash in your face. Don't look directly at the sun. Wear your sunglasses on bright days—even in the winter. Now you're lookin' good!

27

Thanks for seeing the sights with me. There's plenty more I'd like to show you about eyes and sight.

I'd like to explore the woods at night. We could discover how cats see in the dark to find food and stay safe. Or we could soar into the sky with an eagle. It can spot a fish in a lake from hundreds of feet off the ground.

For now, remember that seeing is your window to a beautiful world. It's a truly sensational sense. See you soon!

"SEE" YOUR BLIND SPOT

Everyone has a tiny blind spot in each eye. It's where your eye can't catch the light. Find yours!

Prop this book up against a wall. Stand or sit about 20 inches (50 cm) away from it. Cover your right eye, and look at the plus sign with your left eye. You should still see the dot out of the corner of your eye.

Move slowly toward the book. Stop when the dot disappears. You've found the blind spot in your left eye!

Now find it in your right eye. Cover your left eye. This time, focus on the circle. Can you find your blind spot?

●   +

GLOSSARY

Braille (BRAYL): Braille is a system of writing with raised bumps that is read by touch. People who are blind use Braille to read.

communicate (kuh-MYOO-nuh-kayt): To communicate means to share information, thoughts, ideas, or feelings with others. Seeing helps people communicate.

cornea (KOR-nee-uh): The cornea is the clear outer layer of the eye. The cornea helps your eye focus.

focus (FOH-kuss): To focus means to adjust to see clearly. The cornea and lens help your eye focus.

iris (EYE-riss): The iris is the colored part of your eye. The iris changes the size of the pupil to protect the eye.

lens (LENZ): The lens is a clear, flexible part inside the eye. The lens helps your eye focus.

nerves (NURVS): Nerves are pathways that carry messages to or from the brain. Nerves carry messages about the things you see to the brain.

pupil (PYOO-pul): A pupil is the black opening of the eye that lets light in. The pupil changes size depending on darkness and brightness.

retina (RET-un-uh): The retina is the thin layer on the back of the eyeball. The retina has millions of sensors that are sensitive to light.

sense organs (SENSS OR-gins): Sense organs are body parts such as ears, eyes, nose, tongue, and skin that help you understand your world. The eyes are sense organs.

sensors (SEN-surs): Sensors are things that detect heat, pressure, or sight. Sensors in your eyes allow you to see.

FURTHER READING

Collins, Andrew. *See, Hear, Smell, Taste, and Touch: Using Your Five Senses.* Washington DC: National Geographic, 2006.

Walker, Richard. *Eyewitness Human Body.* New York: DK Publishing, 2009.

Weiss, Ellen. *The Sense of Sight.* New York: Children's Press, 2009.

WEB SITES

Visit our Web site for links about your sensational sense of sight:

childsworld.com/links

Note to Parents, Teachers, and Librarians: We routinely verify our Web links to make sure they are safe and active sites. So encourage your readers to check them out!

WITHDRAWN

11/12 - 5

**Indianapolis
Marion County
Public Library**

**Renew by Phone
269-5222**

**Renew on the Web
www.imcpl.org**

For General Library Information
please call 269-1700